The
FRENCH CULTURE
Coloring Book

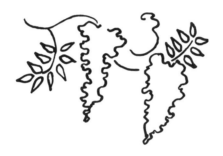

Anne-Françoise Pattis

PASSPORT BOOKS
a division of *NTC Publishing Group*
Lincolnwood, Illinois USA

Published by Passport Books, a division of NTC Publishing Group.
© 1994 by NTC Publishing Group, 4255 West Touhy Avenue,
Lincolnwood (Chicago), Illinois 60646-1975 U.S.A.
Manufactured in the United States of America.

3 4 5 6 7 8 9 0 VP 9 8 7 6 5 4 3 2 1

Table des matières   Contents

Orientation   Overview
La terre dans l'espace   The Earth in Space   3
La France dans le monde   France in the World   4
La France   France   6
Le drapeau français   The French Flag   7

Portraits et paysages   Portraits and Landscapes
Les Français   The French   8
L'Alsace   Alsace   10
La Provence   Provence   11
Les Landes   Landes   12
La Bretagne   Brittany   13
La campagne française   The French Countryside   14
La Côte d'Azur   The French Riviera   16
Les Alpes   The Alps   17
La vigne   Vineyards   18
La vache   Cows   19

Les fêtes   Holidays
Noël   Christmas   20
Epiphanie   Epiphany   21
Mardi Gras   Fat Tuesday   22
Pâques   Easter   23
La Fête des mères   Mother's Day   24
Le 14 juillet   The 14th of July   25

Les courses   Shopping
Le marché en ville   The City Market   26
Le marché au village   The Country Market   27
La boulangerie   The Bakery   28
La fleuriste   The Florist   29
La crémerie   The Dairy Store   30
L'argent français   French Money   31

Histoire de France   French History
La préhistoire   Prehistoric Times   32
Les Gaulois   The Gauls   33
Le Moyen Age   The Middle Ages   34
La Renaissance   The Renaissance   35
Louis XIV   Louis XIV   36

La Révolution française   The French Revolution   37

Le Concorde   The *Concord*   38

Monuments   Monuments

Notre-Dame   Notre Dame Cathedral   39

Un vitrail de Chartres   A Stained Glass Window   40
                             from Chartres

Le Mont-Saint-Michel   Mont-Saint-Michel   41

La tour Eiffel   The Eiffel Tower   42

La pyramide du Louvre   The Louvre Pyramid   43

Une bonne journée   A Nice Day

L'école   School   44

«Le Corbeau et le renard»   "The Fox and the Crow"   45

Le métro   The Subway   46

Les crêpes   Crêpes   47

Le manège   The Merry-Go-Round   48

«Au clair de la lune»   "In the Shining Moonlight"   49

Divertissements   Amusements

La terrasse de café   The Terrace of a Café   50

La pétanque   The Game of Pétanque   51

Giverny   Giverny   52

Le jardin du Luxembourg   The Luxembourg Garden   53

La montgolfière   The First Hot-Air Balloons   54

Guignol   Punch and Judy   55

Pronunciation Guide   56

Notes   57

Orientation

La terre dans l'espace

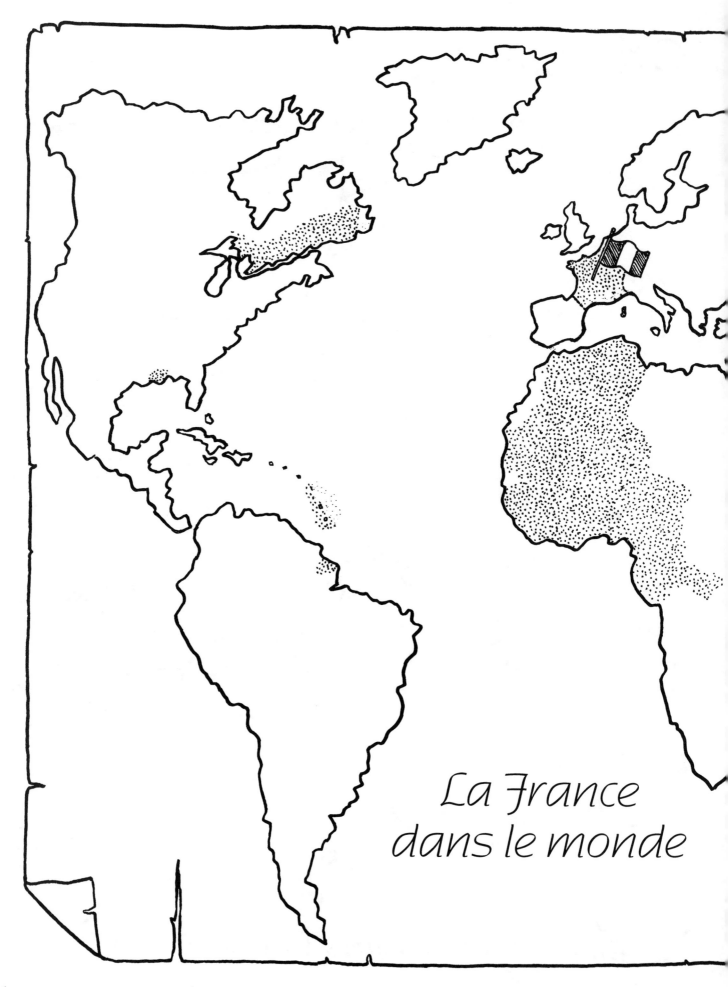

La France
dans le monde

4

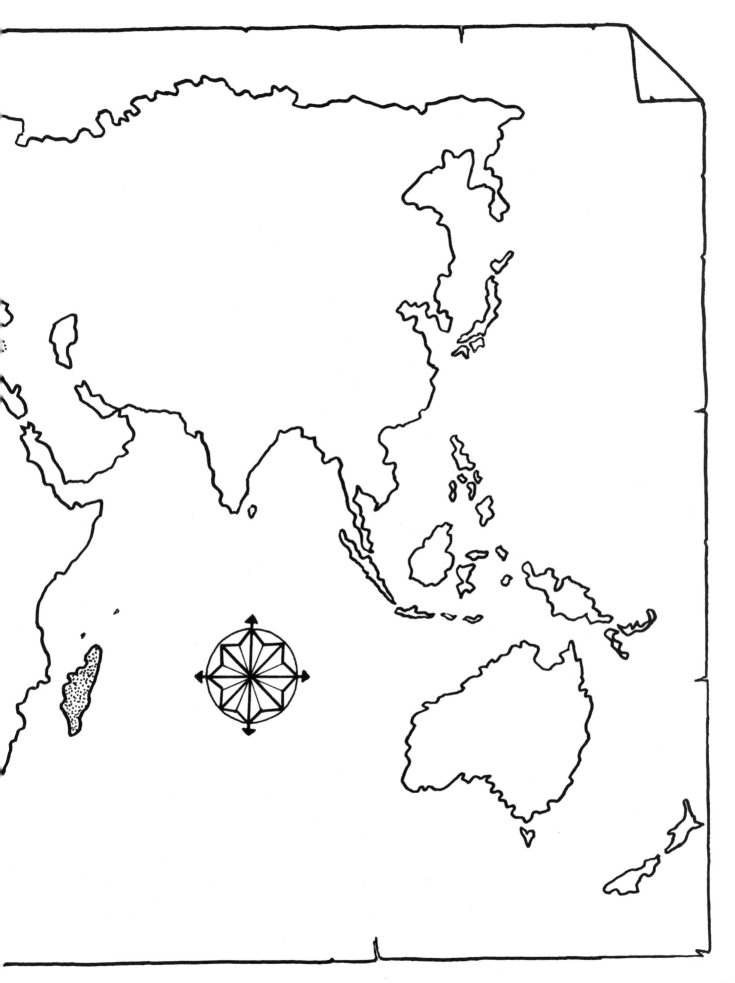

5

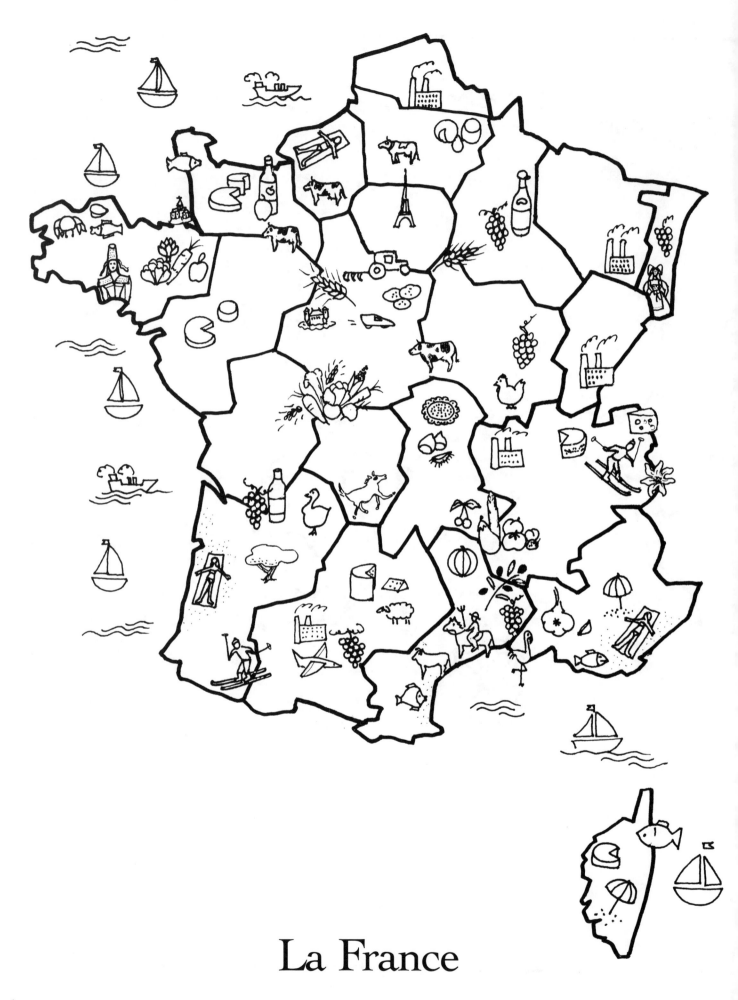

La France

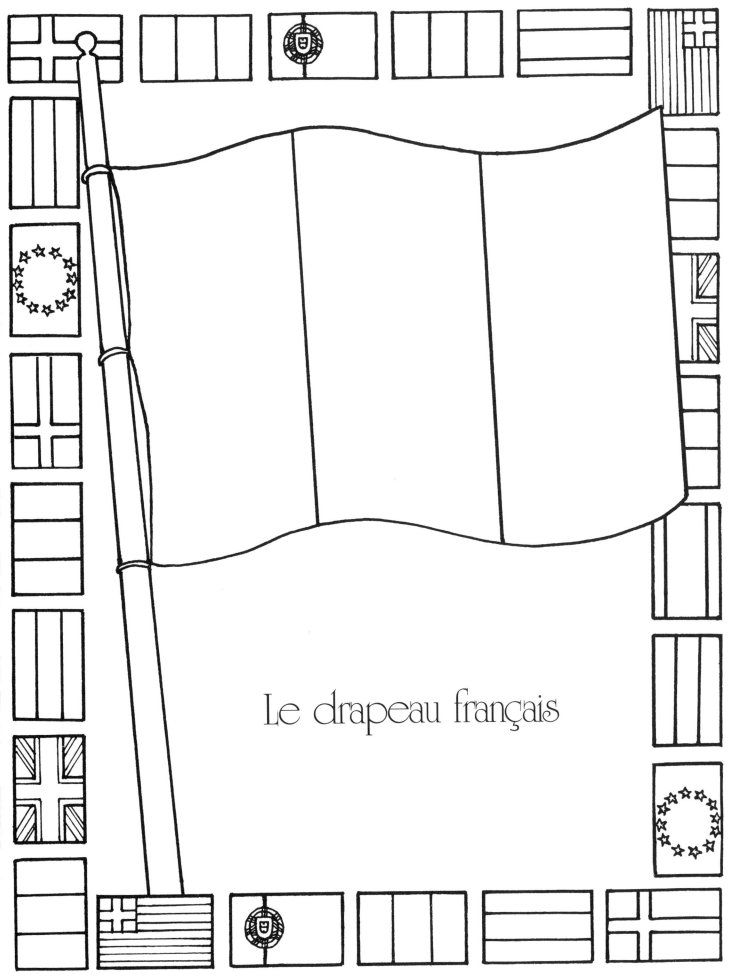

Le drapeau français

Portraits et paysages

Les

Français

L'Alsace

 La Provence

Les Landes

La Bretagne

13

La campagne française

15

La Côte d'Azur

Les Alpes

17

La vigne

La vache

Les fêtes

Santons de Provence

Noël

Epiphanie

21

Mardi Gras

Pâques

La Fête des mères

Le 14 juillet

Les courses

Le marché en ville

Le marché au village

27

La boulangerie

La fleuriste

La crémerie

L'argent français

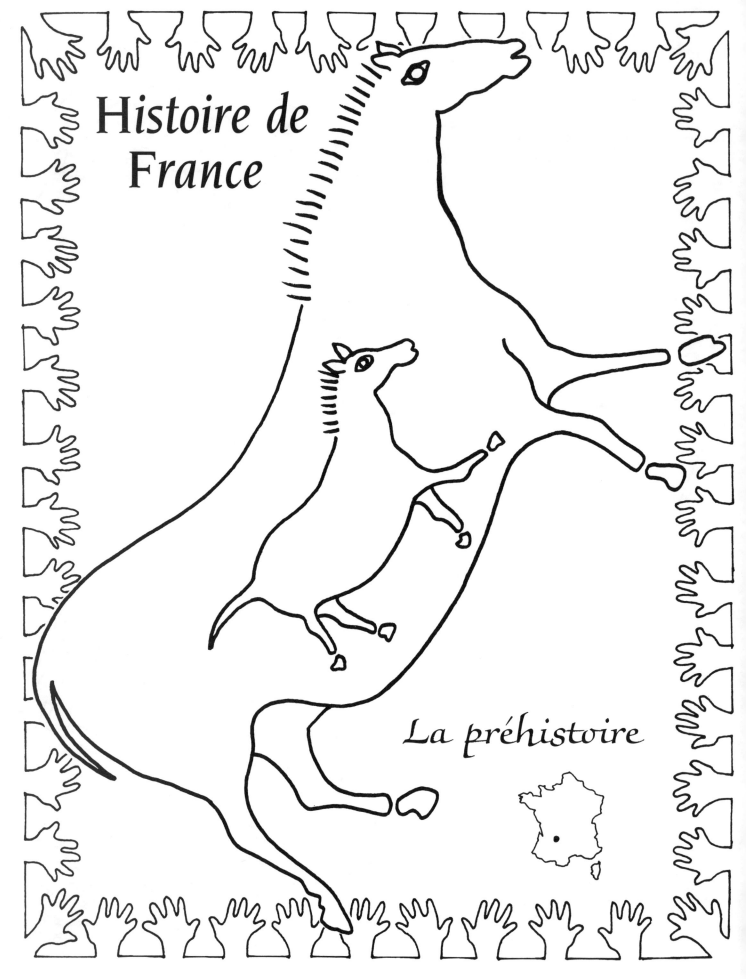

Histoire de France

La préhistoire

Les Gaulois

33

Le Moyen Age

La Renaissance

Louis XIV

La Révolution française

LE CONCORDE

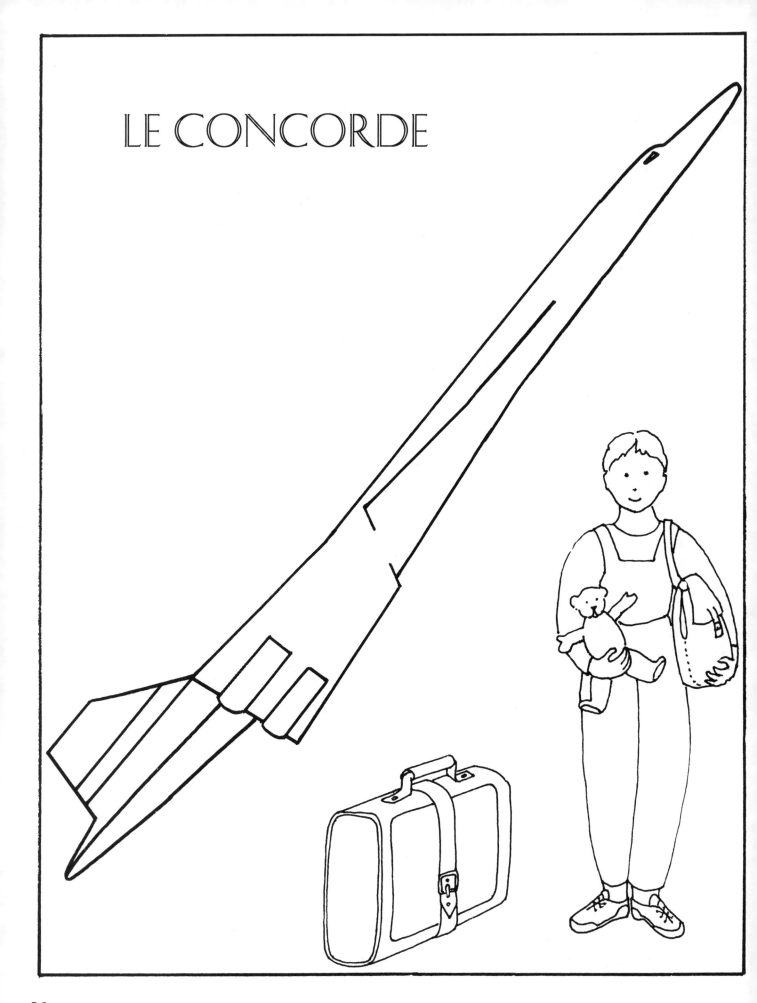

Notre-Dame

Un vitrail de Chartres

Le Mont-Saint-Michel

41

La tour
Eiffel

La pyramide du Louvre

Une bonne journée

L'école

«Le corbeau
et le renard»

Le corbeau et le renard*

Maître corbeau, sur un arbre perché,
Tenait en son bec un fromage ;
Maître renard par l'odeur alléché,
Lui tint à peu près ce langage :
'Hé ! bonjour, Monsieur du Corbeau.
Que vous êtes joli ! que vous me semblez beau !
Sans mentir, si votre ramage
Se rapporte à votre plumage,
Vous êtes le phénix des hôtes de ces bois.'
A ces mots, le corbeau ne se sent pas de joie ;
Et, pour montrer sa belle voix,
Il ouvre un large bec, laisse tomber sa proie.
Le renard s'en saisit, et dit : 'Mon bon monsieur,
Apprenez que tout flatteur
Vit aux dépens de celui qui l'écoute.
Cette leçon vaut bien un fromage sans doute.'
Le corbeau honteux et confus
Jura, mais un peu tard, qu'on ne l'y prendrait plus.

JEAN DE LA FONTAINE

*Translation of poem on p. 56.

Le métro

crêpes

Miel
Beurre
Fromage
Confiture
Sucre

25ᶠ

Les crêpes

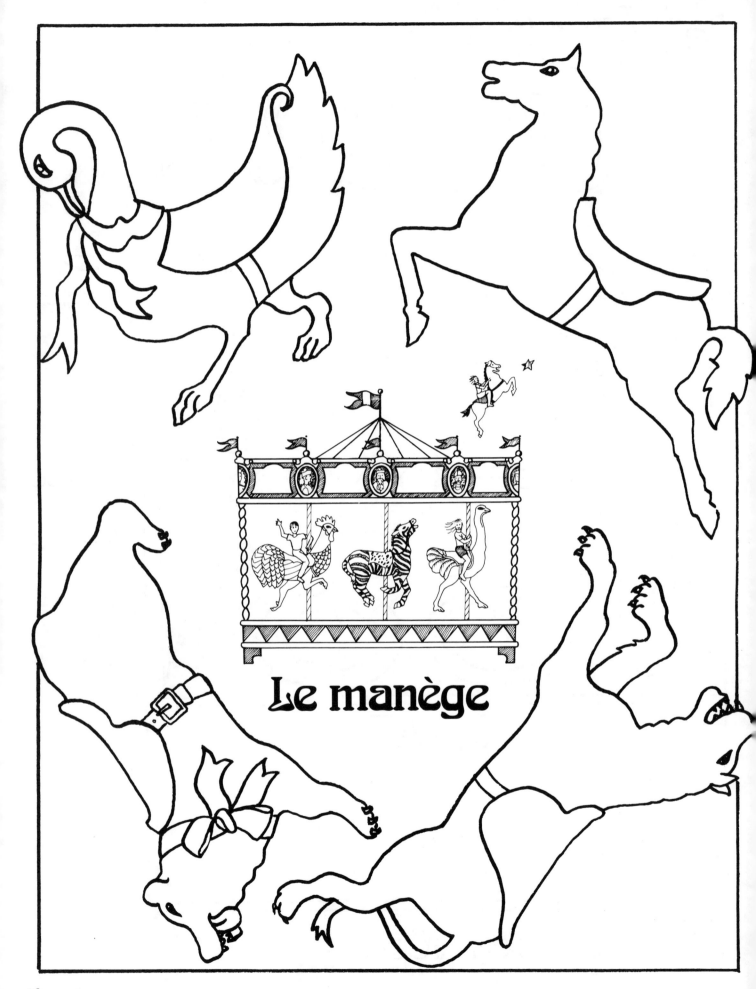

Le manège

48

Au clair de la lune
(Traditional French Folk Song)

Au clair de la lune,
Mon ami Pierrot,
Prête-moi ta plume
Pour écrire un mot;
Ma chandelle est morte,
Je n'ai plus de feu;
Ouvre-moi ta porte,
Pour l'amour de Dieu.

By the Shining Moonlight

By the shining moonlight,
My dear friend Pierrot,
Please lend me your quill pen
To write down a note;
I've burned out my candle,
And my fire's out too;
Pray, open your door, please,
Goodness' sake, now do.

«Au clair de la lune»

Divertissements

La terrasse de café

La pétanque

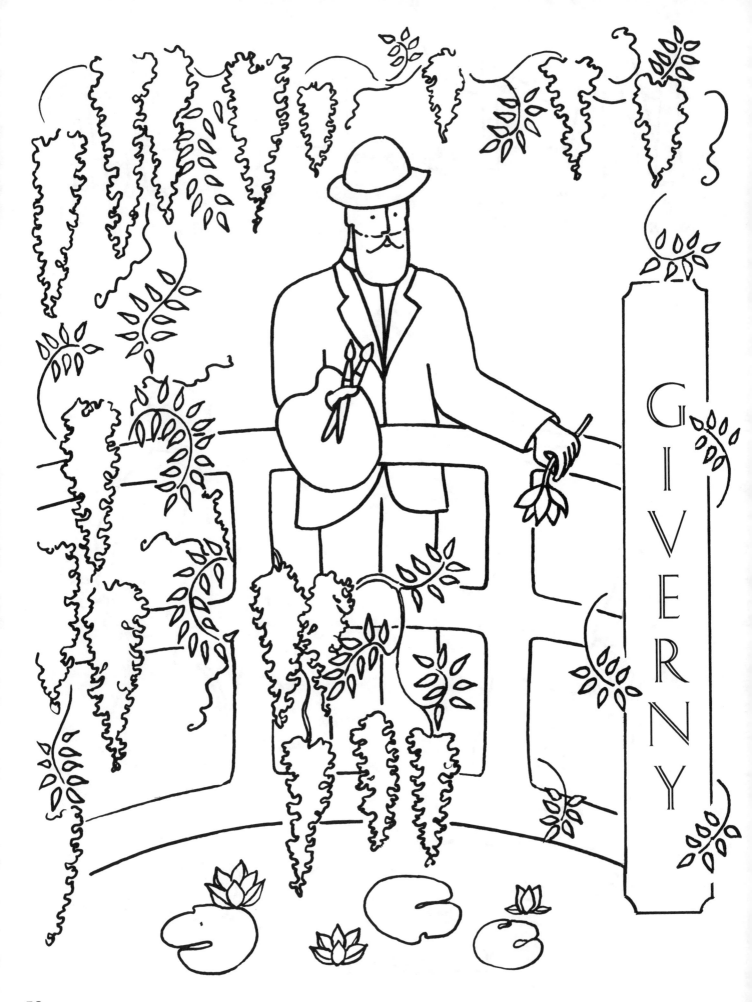

Le jardin du Luxembourg

La montgolfière

Guignol

Pronunciation Guide

Orientation (o-ree-ahn-tah-*syohn*)
La terre dans l'espace (lah tair dahn les-*pahs*)
(p. 3)
La France dans le monde (la frahns dahn luh
mohnd) (p. 4)
La France (la frahns) (p. 6)
Le drapeau français (luh drah-*poh* frahn-*seh*) (p. 7)

Portraits et paysages (por-*treh* ay pay-ee-*zahzh*)
Les Français (lay frahn-*seh*) (p. 8)
L'Alsace (lahl-*zahs*) (p. 10)
La Provence (la proh-*vahns*) (p. 11)
Les Landes (lay lahnd) (p. 12)
La Bretagne (lah bruh-*tah*-nyah) (p. 13)
La campagne française (lah kah-*pah*-nyah
fran-*sehz*) (p. 14)
La Côte d'Azur (lah koht dah-*zoor*) (p. 16)
Les Alpes (layz ahlp) (p.17)
La vigne (lah *vee*-nyah) (p. 18)
La vache (lah vahsh) (p. 19)

Les fêtes (lay fet)
Noël (no-*el*) (p. 20)
Epiphanie (ay-pee-fah-*nee*) (p. 21)
Mardi Gras (mahr-*dee* grah) (p. 22)
Pâques (pahk) (p. 23)
La Fête des mères (lah fet day mair) (p. 24)
Le quatorze juillet (luh kah-*torz* zhwee-*yay*) (p. 25)

Les courses (lay coors)
Le marché en ville (luh mahr-*shay* ahn veel)
(p. 26)
Le marché au village (luh mahr-*shay* oh vee-lazh)
(p. 27)
La boulangerie (lah boo-lahn-zhair-*ee*) (p. 28)
La fleuriste (lah fluhr-*eest*) (p. 29)
La crémerie (lah krehm-*ree*) (p. 30)
L'argent français (lahr-*zhahn* frahn-*seh*) (p. 31)

Histoire de France (ees-*twahr* duh frahns)
La préhistoire (lah pray-ees-*twahr*) (p. 32)
Les Gaulois (lay gohl-*wah*) (p. 33)
Le Moyen Age (luh mwa-*yen* ahzh) (p. 34)
La Renaissance (lah ruh-neh-*sahns*) (p. 35)
Louis XIV (loo-*ee* kah-*torz*) (p. 36)
La Révolution française (lah ray-vo-loo-see-*yohn*
fran-*sehz*) (p. 37)
Le Concorde (luh kohn-*kord*) (p. 38)

Monuments (mohn-oo-*mahn*)
Notre-Dame (*no*-truh dahm) (p. 39)
Un vitrail de Chartres (uhn vee-*trah*-yuh duh
shar-truh) (p. 40)
Le Mont-Saint-Michel (luh mohn san mee-*shel*)
(p. 41)

La tour Eiffel (lah toor ay-*fel*) (p. 42)
La pyramide du Louvre (lah pee-rah-*meed* doo
loo-vruh) (p. 43)

Une bonne journée (oon buhn zhoor-*nay*)
L'école (lay-*kol*) (p. 44)
Le corbeau et le renard (luh kor-*bow* ay luh
run-*ahr*) (p. 45)
Le métro (luh may-*troh*) (p. 46)
Les crêpes (lay krep) (p. 47)
Le manège (luh mahn-*ehzh*) (p. 48)
Au clair de la lune (oh klair duh lah loon) (p. 49)

Divertissements (dee-vair-tees *mahn*)
La terrasse de café (lah tair-*ahs* duh kay-*fay*)
(p. 50)
La pétanque (lah pay-*tahnk*) (p. 51)
Giverny (zhee-vair-*nee*) (p. 52)
Le jardin du Luxembourg (luh zhar-*dan* doo
looks-uhm-*boor*) (p. 53)
La montgolfière (lah mohn-gol-fee-*air*) (p. 54)
Guignol (guee-*nyol*) (p. 55)

The following is a translation of the poem appearing
on page 45.

The Fox and the Crow

Master Crow, perched in a tree,
Was holding a cheese in his beak;
Master Fox, lured by the smell,
Came up and started to speak:
"Ah, good day, Milord Crow.
How handsome you are! You almost glow!
To lie, I need not;
If your singing equals the feathers you've got,
You're the shining star of our woodland home."
At these words, the crow cannot help but rejoice;
And to show the world his beautiful voice,
His beak opens wide and lets fall the cheese, oh so choice.
The fox grabs it and says: "My good Sir,
You should know that every flatterer
Lives off those who gives him heed.
That lesson's worth a cheese. Yes, indeed!"
The crow, ashamed and confused,
Swore (but too late) that never again would he be used.

Notes

These notes give you more information about what you see in the pictures you are coloring. They help you learn many interesting facts about France, the French people, and things you see in France.

Orientation *Overview*

La France dans le monde *France in the World* (Page 4)
France is in Europe. It is on the western tip of the European continent. You cannot go farther west without crossing over water. Because of this, over the ages, as peoples and tribes moved through Europe, many stopped in France. France has six neighbors: Belgium, Luxembourg, Germany, Switzerland, Italy, and Spain. Across the English Channel to the northwest is England.

La France *France* (Page 6)
France has high mountains, flat plains, rolling hills. It has dry areas and wetlands, warm and cool places. There are large cities and tiny villages. France is not a very large country. You can drive from one end to the other in less than a day. The capital of France is Paris.

Le drapeau français *The French Flag* (Page 7)
Through their history, the French had used the colors blue, white, and red on banners and flags. But all three were never together on the same flag until the French Revolution, which began in 1789. (For more about the revolution, see **La Révolution française** on p. 67.) During that troubled time, the king of France, Louis XVI, tried to please all his people. He added a red and blue badge (called a "cockade") to the white badge he was wearing. White was the color of the king, and red and blue were the colors of the revolution. The three colors became the colors of the French flag. Together they show the unity of the French nation.

Portraits et paysages *Portraits and Landscapes*

Les Français *The French* (Page 8)
In France, there are people of different ages, different colors, different shapes, and different religions. The people like to wear different clothes, eat different foods, and do different things for fun. In France, there are about 58 million people. To get an idea of how many people that is, you can compare the number of people in France with the number of people in other countries. Look at the drawing.

India: 900,000,000  United States of America: 250,000,000 France: 57,000,000  Spain: 40,000,000

L'Alsace, La Provence, Les Landes, La Bretagne *Alsace, Provence, Landes, Brittany* (Page 10)
Pages 10 to 13 show traditional costumes from these four provinces of France. Long ago, France was made up of areas called "provinces," and each province has kept its own identity through the centuries. This identity includes the province's special history, geography, stories, costumes, foods, music, architecture, and so on. There is no end to the number of differences. However, if you are from Provence or Alsace, you are still totally French, too. In fact, the differences between the provinces are an important part of France's heritage. The French people feel that it is very important to keep these differences.

Landes

Provence

Bretagne

Alsace

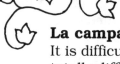

La campagne française *The French Countryside* (Page 14)
It is difficult to describe the French countryside because it looks totally different in different places. The landscape, the trees, and the flowers change as you travel through France. The way people live depends on what the land provides. If there is white stone in the area, then the houses are made of white stones. If there are large trees and not a lot of stones, then the houses are built out of wood.

When you drive through France, you can see many villages with fields, roads, and forests around them. The villages are often very old, and the house are old, too. There is usually an old church in the middle of the village. There is a square where the market has opened once a week for as long as everyone can remember. The streets are usually narrow because they were built long before cars existed. However, the countryside is changing quickly in France. It is becoming more and more modern, but in many places, it still keeps its old charm.

La Côte d'Azur *The French Riviera* (Page 16)
The French Riviera is in southern France on the Mediterranean Sea. There the weather is mild all year round. You can hardly tell it is winter except that the tourists are gone. In February, the mimosa are in bloom. Mimosa are yellow flowers that look like millions of yellow snowflakes as they bloom on trees. Mimosa smell sweet, almost like vanilla. The Riviera is very popular for holidays because it has good beaches and sunshine. It also has both modern cities and old villages to visit. During the summer months, it is a very busy part of France as people from France and other countries travel there for vacation.

Les Alpes   *The Alps* (Page 17)

If you like skiing, climbing, hiking, or looking for rare flowers and wild animals, go to the Alps. In all seasons, the mountains are beautiful. The Alps are the largest and highest mountains in Europe. The tallest mountain in the Alps is called **Le Mont Blanc**. This means "white mountain." Its top is about 15,000 feet up in the sky. From the top, you can see far into France, Italy, and Switzerland.

La vigne   *Vineyards* (Page 18)

Grapes grow all over France, except in the far north where it is too cold and wet. Growing grapes takes a great deal of work and care. People have to cut and tie the vines. They also have to plow the land and spray the grapes. And in the fall, there is the harvest. Harvesting is often done by hand, and each bunch of grapes is picked one at a time. Grapes come in many colors and flavors. They are used to make wine or grape juice. They are also eaten fresh for dessert or as a snack.

   Vineyards are very nice to look at because they are very orderly. The plants are evenly spaced out in long rows. They have large green leaves that turn red in the fall.

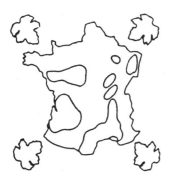

La vache   *Cows* (Page 19)

In France, you can see plains with cows, hills with cows, and mountains with cows. They are everywhere, except in cities and in the far south, where it is too dry to grow grass to feed them. In France, there is one cow for every three people! What do cows give us? They give us milk and meat, of course. The cows eat grass in the fields all day, and in the evening, they go back to the farm to be milked. On the farm, there are also other farm animals. There are sheep and goats, pigs and horses. Look at the drawing. Which group has the largest number of animals? Which group has the least number of animals?

Les fêtes *Holidays*

Noël *Christmas (Page 20)*

It is a clear December night in the south of France. The village drummer plays loudly to tell the happy news. All the villagers are coming. Adults, children, and animals gather around the stable to worship the baby Jesus. Many bring simple gifts. A shepherd comes from the hills with his dog and his sheep. He wears a long cape and a wide hat. The miller is on his way from his mill with a sack of flour. The fish seller carries fish in a basket. A woman brings fruit. A young man carries a lamb. The man with his arms up in the air is overjoyed at this pretty sight.

For all these people in their small village of Provence, it is a happy night. But would you believe that each of them is smaller than the palm of your hand? They are dolls made out of clay and painted by hand. They are part of a nativity scene, called a **crèche**. The **crèche** is just one of the Christmas traditions in France. Children enjoy putting out **crèches** in their homes and listening to traditional stories. Do you know of any other holiday traditions? All of us have some, no matter what religion we believe in. Which holiday traditions do you like best?

Epiphanie *Epiphany (21)*

This holiday is on January 6. It takes place 12 days after Christmas. It is about the arrival of the three wise kings, who came from faraway lands to see the baby Jesus. For the Christmas **crèche**, the three kings are also made into clay dolls, and they are put out on the first Sunday of the new year. On this day, the family shares a special dessert called a **galette des rois**. A **galette** is a flat round cake. It is made of a special dough and often stuffed with an almond filling. The most interesting part is that there is something hidden inside the cake. The baker hides a **fève** in it. What's a **fève**? It's a lima bean—in this case, a dried lima bean. The cake is cut into slices, and everyone bites into his or her slice very carefully. Each person hopes to find the **fève**. If the **fève** is in your slice, you are the queen or the king for the day and you are crowned with a gold paper crown. You also will have good luck during the new year. **Fèves** may also be porcelain and come in different shapes. Look at the most popular shapes around this note.

Mardi Gras *Fat Tuesday* (Page 22)

Mardi Gras means "Fat Tuesday." It is the Tuesday before Lent. You may know that Lent is the season of fasting and penance before Easter. But Fat Tuesday is a day to eat lots of good food and to have fun. The tradition is for people to celebrate and make noise to scare evil spirits away. People dress up in costumes, and they sing and dance in the streets. Some French cities, such as Nice in the South, have carnivals and parades at the time of **Mardi Gras**.

Sometimes schools have parties. After school, children parade through the streets in their costumes, ring door bells, and ask for candy. When they go home, they have a snack of **crêpes** (sweet pancakes) or **beignets** (sweet rolls fried like doughnuts). These are two sweet dishes traditionally served at **Mardi Gras**.

Pâques *Easter* (Page 23)

At Eastertime, bakeries display delicious-looking chocolate eggs, as well as chocolate fish, lambs, and hens. The large chocolates have big yellow, blue, and pink bows tied around them. They are hollow, and, when you crack them open, out come small sugar eggs. One Easter tradition is for children to hunt for eggs in their backyards. A legend says that 40 days before Easter, all church bells in France go to Rome. On Easter morning, the bells fly home, dropping candy eggs as they go. At the same time, they ring a happy tune in the spring sky to announce the resurrection of Christ. On Easter, French families get together and share a lunch of roast lamb.

La Fête des mères *Mothers' Day* (Page 24)

In France, Mothers' Day takes place on the last Sunday in the month of May. In school, young children design special cards for their mothers with the help of their teachers. Many mothers receive flowers from their children. Mothers' Day is the day when mothers are honored for the important achievement of raising families. On that day, the French show their appreciation of their mothers.

Le 14 juillet *The 14th of July (Bastille Day)* (Page 25)

July 14th is the French national holiday. There are fireworks and dances in the street. There is a big parade in Paris, with planes flying in the sky. On this day, the French people remember the Great Revolution. This was the beginning of democracy in France and the idea that all people were free and equal. (For more about this, see **La Révolution française** on p. 67.) The holiday recalls the day on which French people took over a prison called the Bastille. In English, it is also called Bastille Day. Nowadays **le 14 juillet** is a very happy and noisy celebration.

61

Les courses   *Shopping*

Les marchés   *Markets* (Pages 26 & 27)

Market day in a French town is unlike any other day. It is an exciting and busy day. People come from all over the area to buy food and goods. It takes place every week, on the same morning, at the same place. It usually takes place outdoors. A market is filled with colors and noises. There you can buy the freshest foods. There are sweets and breads and cheeses and fruits and vegetables and fish and meat. There are also flowers and seedlings and baskets and clothes and even some things you may not expect. After we buy what we want, the only problem is carrying everything home. On the way, we can watch other people and listen to the street musicians.

La boulangerie   *The Bakery* (Page 28)

A French baker gets up very early so that customers can have hot bread (**pain**) fresh from the oven every morning. The bread is crispy on the outside and soft on the inside. The French have bread with every meal. What French children like most of all is to stop at the bakery on their way home from school. There they buy a **petit pain au chocolat** (small roll with chocolate inside) for their **goûter** (afternoon snack). If you don't have a **boulangerie** nearby, you can bake your own **petit pain au chocolat**. Here's how:

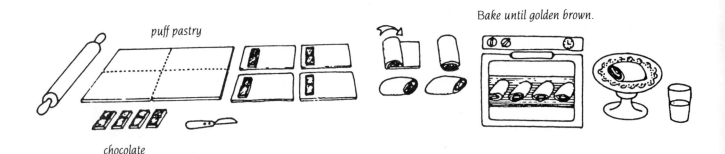

puff pastry

chocolate

Bake until golden brown.

La fleuriste   *The Florist* (Page 29)

The florist in the drawing sells fresh flowers from a cart in the street. She does this even in the winter. French people are very fond of flowers. They buy flowers from carts (like the one the florist has), from flower shops, and from outdoor markets. French people love to have flowers in their homes. They like to give flowers as gifts. It is a tradition to bring flowers when they go to a friend's house for dinner. You already know the name of one flower in French because it is just like English: **une rose**, which means "a rose." Florist shops bring the beauty of the country into the busy cities. The flowers are displayed on the sidewalks and in store windows. People who walk by slow down to admire them.

La crémerie   *The Dairy Store* (Page 30)

At the **crémerie**, the French can buy hundreds of delicious foods made with milk. The **crémerie** sells milk, of course, and there are also butter and cream and yogurt and a great variety of cheeses. Cheese can be mild or strong-tasting, soft or hard, sweet or salty, large or small, white or yellow or orange or even blue. Over 350 kinds of cheese are made in France. The cheeses are made from cows' milk, goats' milk, and ewes' milk (ewes are female sheep). Most French people eat cheese every day. They eat it with crusty bread at the end of a meal, right before dessert.

Cheeses—large and small

The salesperson at the **crémerie** in the drawing wears a white uniform, a white apron, and a small white hat. She cuts the cheese with a large knife to give customers the exact amount they want. Then she puts the piece on a sheet of paper, and she weighs it to find out the price. In the drawing, you can see many cheeses on display in the **crémerie**. Notice that the word **crémerie** has the word **crème** in it. **Crème**, as you may guess, means "cream."

L'argent français   *French Money* (Page 31)

French money is called the **franc**. Francs come in coins and in bills. There are several different sizes of coins. For example, there are coins of 1 franc, 2 francs, 5 francs, 10 francs, and 20 francs, besides smaller coins. The bills also come in different sizes and they are colorful. On each bill is the picture of a famous French person. It may be of a writer, a painter, or a musician.

Histoire de France   French History

La préhistoire   *Prehistoric Times* (Page 32)

In prehistoric times, ice covered the northern part of France. In the southern part of the country, people lived by fishing and hunting. In bad weather, they would stay in caves. On the walls of some of these caves, they painted the animals that they hunted. Their art may also have been a part of their religion. They painted bison, mammoths (a kind of large elephant now extinct), reindeer, and horses. Sometimes the artists would also leave a picture of their hands, by placing one of their hands on the wall of the cave and splashing paint around it.

The pictures in the drawing were painted long, long ago. They were made 20,000 years ago. Here is a way for you to understand how long ago that is. If you have a new pencil, hold it in front of you. Imagine that the length of the tip (which is rather short) represents our history going back from our time to 0 A.D. This is around 2,000 years. The rest of the pencil, after the tip to the eraser, represents the time between 0 A.D. and the period when prehistoric artists painted the walls of their caves. Isn't it amazing that today you can look at the horse and still know what it is and appreciate its beauty?

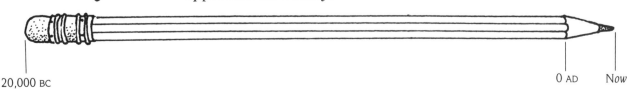

20,000 BC

0 AD   Now

Les Gaulois   *The Gauls* (Page 33)

The Celts were people who came from the east looking for new land. They invaded Western Europe around 3,000 years ago. After they arrived, some of them decided to stay in France, and they were later called "the Gauls." **La Gaule** was the old name for France. The Gauls were good warriors, but they were also good farmers. They turned bad land into farmland, and they built roads and harbors. Priests played an important role in the life of the Gauls. These priests were called "Druids." The Druids were also teachers and judges, and they were powerful in politics. Today French children spend a lot of time studying the history of the Gauls. This is because French people have long thought of the Gauls as their ancestors.

Le Moyen Age   *The Middle Ages* (Page 34)

The Middle Ages was the time of knights in suits of armor, dark castles, deep forests, princes and princesses, and fairy tales. The Middle Ages in French history covers 1,000 years, from the fifth century to the fifteenth century. It is also called "feudal times." At that time, France was controlled by many chiefs who fought long wars against each other. It was a time of fear and misery for most people.

Today, we can still see the wonderful art of this colorful period. There are hundreds of churches, cathedrals, and monasteries in France. Many of them are still decorated with their original stained-glass windows and sculptures. From this period, we also have funny stories that make fun of people. In some of these, animals, including the fox and the wolf, are used to make fun of the way people act. There are also handwritten books with decorated letters, as well as music and tapestries, like the one in this drawing.

Children in France study this period in detail in order to understand their history. But it is easy to spend many hours on such a mysterious period.

La Renaissance   *The Renaissance* (Page 35)

Renaissance means "rebirth." The drawing shows the castle of Azay-le-Rideau in the Loire Valley, in north central France. It was built between 1518 and 1528, at the time of the Renaissance. The castles of the Middle Ages had been built as fortresses for protection in war, but the castles of Renaissance were built as elegant and comfortable homes. Azay-le-Rideau is no longer dark like a medieval fortress. Instead, it has tall windows that open out on to a beautiful park. During the period of the Renaissance, the French rediscovered the beauty of Italy and of ancient Rome. They became interested in all forms of art that celebrated the beauty of nature. In the Middle Ages, art had been used to praise God. Now art showed the beauty of nature and humanity.

Louis XIV   *Louis XIV* (Page 36)

Louis XIV lived from 1643 to 1715. He was the most powerful of the French monarchs. He called himself the Sun King because he saw himself as shining over his entire kingdom. Everyone lived in his light. He obeyed no one except God. He built a beautiful palace at Versailles. This palace was a place to show off his glory and power. All the nobles in the land were expected to live at Versailles and to serve the king. All of the king's life was turned into a ceremony. For the king, just getting out of bed lasted two hours. It was considered a great honor to attend this ceremony. During Louis's long reign, France achieved great things, but the country also saw terrible misery and loss of freedom.

La Révolution française   *The French Revolution* (Page 37)

In 1789, when Louis XVI was king of France, the French Revolution began. For a long time, the French people had paid many taxes. Some were starving while the rich nobles lived well. The most famous event in the revolution took place in Paris on July 14, 1789, when a crowd of angry Parisians took over the Bastille. The Bastille was a prison that was a symbol of the power of the king. Later that same year, the Declaration of the Rights of Man was written and adopted. (Women's rights are more recent.) This document declared the freedom and equality of all citizens. Within three years, the first Republic was set up, and soon after that, the king's head was cut off. The French Revolution was a time of great violence and great changes. It was the beginning of equality in France, but there were many more revolts and wars before democracy became strong in France.

Le Concorde   *The Concorde* (Page 38)

The **Concorde** is a supersonic jet. This means it flies faster than sound moves. It is built by French and British companies, and it is the fastest airplane that carries passengers. With the **Concorde**, Paris is only 3½ hours from New York or Washington. This is about half the time on a regular airplane. The **Concorde** began service in 1979. It is an example of what modern French science and technology can do.

Monuments   *Monuments*

Notre Dame   *Notre Dame Cathedral* (Page 39)

Notre Dame is a Catholic cathedral. It is built on an island in the River Seine. It is in the exact center of Paris, and all distances from Paris are measured from it. Notre Dame gives you a good idea of what French churches and other buildings looked like in the Middle Ages. (For more about the Middle Ages, see **Le Moyen Age** on page 66.) The style of Notre Dame is called "Gothic." Gothic buildings are made of stone and glass. They are held up on the outside by stone pillars (posts) called "buttresses." This way, there could be many windows in the walls. The walls did not have to be made of thick stone to hold up the roof. There are often large round stained-glass windows in Gothic buildings called "rose windows."

Notre Dame was one of the first Gothic buildings. Inside, the cathedral is all lit up by the colored light that comes through the stained glass. From outside, the cathedral seems to be floating on the Seine River like a giant sailboat.

Glass blowing

Un vitrail de Chartres   *A Stained Glass Window from Chartres* (Page 40)

In the Middle Ages, glassmakers did not know how to make large flat sheets of glass like the ones we have in our windows today. Instead, they made small disks of glass. They would then put the pieces of glass together to make a large window. The pieces were held together with strips of lead. The first glass was greenish-gray, but later the glassmakers created a wide variety of bright colors. That let them design windows with colorful patterns like the one in the drawing. The drawing shows a very famous stained-glass window in the Cathedral of Chartres, near Paris. Chartres is considered the most beautiful of all cathedrals by many people. The stained glass shows an episode from the childhood of Jesus— the flight into Egypt. This stained glass was made in about 1150.

Le Mont-Saint-Michel   *Mont Saint Michel* (Page 41)

Mont Saint Michel (Saint Michael's Mount) is one of the most popular tourist sights in France. It is in Normandy, in the northwestern part of France. It is a very large abbey—a monastery with a church—built in the Middle Ages. It sits on the rocky tip of a thin piece of land that sticks out into the water. The strip of land that connects it to the mainland is covered by water when the tide is high. When the tide comes in, Mont Saint Michel looks like an island. For this reason, the monastery was safe from invasions when it was built. Nowadays, however, Mont Saint Michel is invaded daily—by tourists.

La tour Eiffel   *The Eiffel Tower* (Page 42)

The Eiffel Tower is 984 feet high. It was built in 1889 for a large trade fair. It was not made to be admired for its beauty. It is built entirely of metal to show off France's achievements in science and technology. At the time it was put up, it was the tallest building in the world. Surprisingly, once the fair was over, the building was not torn down, and it has become a famous Parisian sight. In fact, to many, it is the symbol of Paris—and of France. From the top of the tower, the view over Paris is fantastic. Visitors can take an elevator almost to the top, and they can walk up the rest of the way.

La pyramide du Louvre   *The Louvre Pyramid* (Page 43)

The pyramid of the Louvre was opened in 1989. It is really the entrance to the Louvre Museum. It is made of glass and metal, and you can see right through it. The pyramid looks most beautiful at night. Then it is lit from the inside and glows brightly in the dark. Many Parisians dislike the pyramid. They think that it spoils the beauty of the historical buildings around it. On the other hand, many other people think it is beautiful. The architect who designed it is I. M. Pei, an American born in China. Because of pollution, the pyramid has to be completely washed every month. When you go down inside the pyramid, you find a marble hall with shops, a restaurant, and the entrances to all of the parts of the Louvre Museum. Much work is being done to make the Louvre Museum more modern. When all the work is completed, the museum will be the largest in the world.

La Joconde

Une bonne journée   A Nice Day

L'école   *School* (Page 44)

In France, children must go to school from the age 6 to the age of 16, but most children start nursery school at the age of 3. Kindergarten, grammar school, high school, and college are paid for by the government, and all children can go to school for free. The schools throughout France teach the same program at the same speed. To go to a university, students have to pass an exam called the **baccalauréat**. They have to get a grade of at least 12 out of 20 points. In France, grades for tests and exams go from 0 to 20, which is the highest.

Le métro   *The Subway* (Page 46)

The subway, or **métro**, of Paris was opened in 1900. Nowadays it has many electric trains that run mostly underground. Taking the métro is quiet and convenient. There are stops all over Paris. The price of a ticket is the same whether you go a long distance or only a short one. When you stand on the platform to wait for a train, there is a lot going on around you. The walls are covered with advertising. You can learn about what is going on in Paris— concerts, plays, sports events. Often there are people playing music and asking for money. Sometimes you'll see homeless people because it is safe and warm in the subway. During rush hour, the subways are very crowded, but the Parisians are used to the crowds. Four million passengers take the métro each day.

The drawing shows one type of subway entrance. There are many entrances similar to this one. They were designed by an architect named Hector Guimard in the early 1900s. You can see how they copy the curving shapes of plants and flowers. Guimard's entrances are historical monuments. This means that they are protected by the government and they cannot be changed or destroyed.

Les crêpes   *Crêpes* (Page 47)

Crêpes are delicious. They are large thin pancakes. You can buy them on the streets of the city. The crêpe seller cooks your crêpe right in front of you. He pours a lot of crêpe batter on to a hot plate, and after a minute, he flips it over. When it is ready, he spreads butter, jam, honey, or chocolate over it. Then he folds it up inside a sheet of paper, and he hands it to you steaming hot. Crêpes were first made in Brittany, which is in the northwest corner of France. (For more about **Les crêpes**, see **Mardi Gras** on p. 63 and the picture for **La Bretagne** on p. 10.) They are a traditional dish in that province.

Le manège   *The Merry-Go-Round* (Page 48)

In France, as in other countries, the merry-go-round goes around and around. For a few francs, you can ride on an ostrich, a zebra, a bear, or a tiger. You go around and up and down as the organ music is playing. It is very exciting, and as it goes faster, you can almost think that you are riding up into the sky all the way above the city. But after a few days, the wooden animals are packed up, and the merry-go-round moves to another city for other children to enjoy.

Divertissements   *Amusements*

La terrasse de café   *The Terrace of a Café* (Page 50)

French cities are famous for their cafés. A café is different from a restaurant. It serves mainly drinks like coffee, tea, and hot chocolate, as well as ice cream, sandwiches, and light meals. In the summertime, cafés have tables outside on the sidewalk. You can sit under the shade of a large umbrella and enjoy ice cream, fruit juice, soft drinks, or lemonade. In the winter, the café is a good place to warm up and have a hot drink like tea or hot cocoa. A café is a great place to relax or read. But everyone would agree that the most interesting thing to do in a café is to watch people walk by on the street.

La pétanque   *The Game of Pétanque* (Page 51)

Let's start a game of *pétanque*. First, find a flat open area. Then one of the players throws a small wooden ball out from the throwing line. Wherever the ball falls, it becomes the target. After that, players take turns to throw their ball as close as possible to the target. The balls are made of iron. They are heavy and hard to throw accurately. Any small stone or any bump on the field makes the game more difficult. The player who can get his or her ball closest to the target wins the game. Pétanque started in Provence, in the south of France. (For more about **La pétanque**, see the picture for **La Provence** on p. 10.) There it is usually played in a shady area. It is a great game if you wish to stay outside and visit with friends. It is not a game of strength and does not take a lot of effort. This is a good thing because it is often very hot in the south of France.

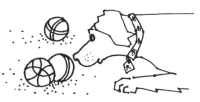

Giverny   *Giverny* (Page 52)

Giverny is a French village, not far from Paris. It is where the painter Claude Monet lived and worked from 1883 until his death in 1926. Monet was a famous painter. His paintings, with many bright colors, are filled with light. Monet's house at Giverny is famous for its beautiful flower garden. Monet used the garden in his paintings. He created a lovely pond with a bridge over it. Monet loved to paint water lilies, and these flowers are still growing there. Nowadays, Monet's house and garden are a museum, and everyone can enjoy their beauty, especially in the early summer when many of the flowers are in bloom.

Le jardin du Luxembourg   *The Luxembourg Garden* (Page 53)

The Luxembourg Garden is in Paris. It is a beautiful French-style garden. That means that in this garden, many of the trees and bushes are in nice, neat rows. It has long straight paths with lots of trees. It has flower beds and many small lawns where no one is allowed to walk. Around the garden are stone sculptures of historic figures. Many people come to the garden, which is surrounded by busy Paris streets. People sit on the chairs along the sides of the lawn, or they stroll down the paths. Joggers run along the paths in the gardens. Children like to meet at the pond and sail toy sailboats. If you don't have a boat of your own, you can rent one from a lady by the pond. In the garden, you can take pony and donkey rides. There is also the famous Guignol Theater, where you can see puppet shows. (For more about this puppet show, see **Guignol** on p. 72 and the picture for **Guignol** on p. 55.) A visit to the Luxembourg Garden can be relaxing, and the garden is very beautiful in the fall when the ground is covered with leaves.

La montgolfière   *The First Hot-Air Balloons* (Page 54)

The word **montgolfière** means a hot-air balloon, and it comes from the name of the two brothers who built the first one in the 1780s. The brothers' names were Joseph-Michel Montgolfier and Jacques-Etienne Montgolfier. They were papermakers, and so the first balloons were made of paper with some cloth. In November 1783, in front of King Louis XVI, Queen Marie-Antoinette, and thousands of people, the Montgolfiers' balloon with two brave men aboard completed the first free flight in history. It lasted 25 minutes.

Guignol   *Punch and Judy* (Page 55)

The Guignol theater is a puppet show. It first started in Italy, and it came to France for the first time in 1795, where it became very popular. This kind of puppet show is known in English-speaking countries as Punch and Judy. Guignol is a funny character, but he is not especially nice. He does not obey rules and is always in trouble with the law. But his actions, especially when he gets into trouble, always make the children in the audience laugh.